How to
Climb
Everest

Born in 1970 in the Solukhumbu district of Nepal, Kami Rita Sherpa is a Nepali guide who had scaled Mount Everest for the first time by the age of twenty-four. He now holds the record for most ascents to the summit, and in May 2019 he scaled the mountain for the twenty-fourth time. He lives with his wife and children in Kathmandu.

Other titles in the series:

How to Play the Piano by James Rhodes
How to Land a Plane by Mark Vanhoenacker
How to Be 'Normal' by Daniel Tammet
How to Skim a Stone by Ralph Jones
How to Enjoy Poetry by Frank Skinner

Little Ways
to live a
Big Life

How to
Climb
Everest

Kami Rita Sherpa

Quercus

First published in Great Britain in 2020 by

Quercus Editions Ltd
Carmelite House
50 Victoria Embankment
London EC4Y 0DZ
An Hachette UK company

A CIP catalogue record for this book is available from the British Library.

ISBN 978 1 52940 961 1
Ebook ISBN 978 1 52940 960 4

10 9 8 7 6 5 4 3 2 1

Illustration by Amber Anderson
Text designed and typeset by CC Book Production
Printed and bound in Great Britain by Clays Ltd, Elcograf S.p.A.

Papers used by Quercus Editions Ltd are from well-managed forests
and other responsible sources.

Contents

Introduction: My Everest World   1

Chapter One: What Does 'Climbing' Mean?   9

Chapter Two: The Challenge   17

Chapter Three: Preparing for Everest   29

Chapter Four: The Climb   39

Notes   53

INTRODUCTION

My Everest World

Even after so many years, the view from the summit is still out of this world: vast, jagged mountains everywhere, columns of cloud bubbling high into the atmosphere and to the north the vast, brown plateau of Tibet. Some of the highest mountains in the world are all around: Lhotse, close by on the other side of the South Col.[1] Makalu to the south-east. Further east, the world's third-highest peak, Kangchenjunga. And they're all below me. The climbers I'm guiding are overjoyed: so many years of dreaming and training towards this moment and now it's come true. Seeing their reaction is absolutely the best part of my job, even better than the spectacular landscape around me.

What I can't see from the summit is my home village of Thame, but I know it's not far: twenty miles or so. When I was a boy, my brother Lhakpa and I would bunk off school and scramble up the little mountain behind the village, called Sunder Peak. We pretended we were like the men we knew who went climbing with the foreigners. So many famous Sherpas have come from Thame. Tenzing Norgay[2] lived there and our heroes Ang Rita and Apa, both record-holders in their time, were born there. They helped make the Sherpa people famous around the world and we wanted to be like them. Now I am in my fiftieth year and celebrating my twenty-fourth ascent of the world's highest mountain: a world record. It's the second time I've climbed Everest in a week. Middle age is not so bad.

We didn't want to climb for the sake of it, my brother and I. We didn't have that luxury. Our house in Thame was one big room that we shared with our parents and six sisters. When the British came to climb Everest almost seventy years ago, with Tenzing Norgay in charge of the Sherpas, our dad Mingma Tsering – who is still alive at a hundred and two – was hired as a

4

porter and carried a load to base camp. For a while he and our mother, Pasang Diki – now eighty-nine – lived in Darjeeling as migrant workers. This is where two of my sisters were born, but then life got too difficult for my grandparents managing the family's yaks and so my parents came home. Altogether they had eleven children, but three died in infancy: that's how it used to be in Khumbu, the district around Everest where I grew up. Often, Sherpa kids are named for the day of the week they were born on: Nima is Sunday, Dawa is Monday, Mingma is Tuesday and so on. But when a boy dies as an infant, as my brother did, the next boy is given a more humble name, like Kami, which means 'blacksmith', to placate the gods. We add the name 'Rita' too, which signifies that an older brother has passed away. Hence my name: Kami Rita.

When I was eight or nine, I went to school. In fact, I was the first student at the new Thame primary school, which Sir Edmund Hillary's Himalayan Trust built in the village. But it wasn't possible to stay beyond the age of eleven or twelve. There were lots of mouths to feed at home and tourism was starting to boom in Khumbu, so I quit school and started carrying loads for trekking groups, sometimes 30kg, carried in a basket or *doko*. That made me strong. Sometimes I'd bring loads to base camp on the back of my family's yaks. When tourist season was over I'd go to the monastery school in the village. I wanted to learn about Buddhism and thought about becoming a monk, but it was too easy to earn a living from tourism. Slowly I worked my way up the ladder, and by my early twenties was guiding tourists on the smaller peaks in Khumbu. I must have climbed some of them dozens of times. By then, my brother Lhakpa was working on Everest for Alpine Ascents International (AAI), an American company. He came to me and said: 'Why are you working for others? Come and work for me.' For that, and many other reasons, he's my hero.

I went to Everest for the first time in 1992, but it wasn't so easy for a Sherpa to make it to the summit in those days. There weren't so many foreign tourists climbing the mountain then, and fewer opportunities. Unless you'd already climbed Everest, it was tough to get a slot guiding a foreigner to the top. Of course, in those days, companies and wealthy clients offered a bonus for reaching the summit, and everyone wanted that. But in 1994, on my third expedition, I finally got the chance. I remember being at the South Col, the top camp below the summit, so excited that I had finally made it but a little bit anxious too that it wouldn't work out. Luckily it did. Since then I've climbed it another twenty-three times, twenty-four if you include the year I went down to camp two and then came back to the top. The government told me: you have to go all the way down to base camp or it doesn't count. Of course, that's easier to say from an office in Kathmandu.

I was sorry to leave the monastery school, but my family was poor and I had to earn a living: what else could I do? The monks taught me some important lessons though, for life and the mountains. I learned about focus and concentration, about being in the moment and aware of my surroundings. Mountains can prey on your mind, on your courage. When the wind blows hard, which it does often at the South Col, you can feel undermined, even anxious. All that determination you brought with you can start to weaken. The mountains then seem frightening, a little bit evil. But the demons are just in your head: negative emotions. As Reinhold Messner once said: 'Mountains are not fair or unfair, they are just dangerous.'

Climbing Everest isn't complicated. It's not like flying an aircraft, with banks of instruments in front of you. But that's not to say that climbing Everest won't push you to the limit: it's about stamina and resilience, and practical common sense. You will be uncomfortable. It will hurt. You may feel you can't go on. But assuming you're typical, your limits are likely to stretch a lot further than you might imagine. The biggest challenge you face is to understand how hard to push and for how long, always allowing for the fact that how high you get is only half the journey. You have to keep something back to get down – to get home.

If you're willing to accept this challenge, then I can help you meet it. After all, I've been working in the mountains for most of my life.

CHAPTER ONE

What Does 'Climbing' Mean?

The word 'climbing' is more complicated than you might think. To me, it has two meanings. First of all it implies 'ascending': going up. Aircraft climb. Stock markets climb. People who walk up a mountain also climb. Some quite big mountains are more or less hikes. Everest is absolutely not one of them, but Kilimanjaro is. Tens of thousands of people a year climb Africa's highest mountain, mostly because you need only be fit and put one foot in front of the other on a steep trail. It's what's known in the United States as a 'walk-up'.

As it happens, people often misjudge Kilimanjaro, which is why so many need rescuing from it. That's because it's almost 6,000 metres high, a serious altitude with only half the air at sea level, requiring proper acclimatisation. (I'll come to that later.) Lots of people think, because they're in good shape, they won't suffer from altitude, but sometimes it's the fittest people who get into the biggest trouble. When it comes to mountains, humility is everything. And don't forget: Everest is more than *two and a half kilometres* higher. Even so, while Kilimanjaro takes fitness and resilience, if you can hike a steep slope with the aid of ski sticks, then technically you've qualified.

Now, let's think about that second meaning of the word 'climbing'. This one covers the different activities that make up the *sport* of climbing, most obviously rock climbing, snow and ice climbing, and mountaineering. Rock climbing happens on steep or even overhanging cliffs. These can be thousands of feet of high, or boulders not much taller than the climber – and everything in between. It's all about hands and feet and body position: a graceful, gymnastic exercise. Mostly, on anything involving any height, climbers use ropes to protect themselves. There's only a bit of scrambling on Everest, but learning how to do easy rock climbs is a great way to learn how to move comfortably on steep ground and keep yourself safe with a rope.

Snow and ice climbing require ice axes in your hands and crampons, essentially spikes, clamped to your boots to tackle steep snow slopes or vertical frozen waterfalls. It takes a while to become practised using this gear. At first, just walking in crampons and clumpy mountaineering boots requires concentration, so you don't spike your ankles and trip over. Do that on a glacier and you could end up falling down a crevasse. You'll have learned some useful skills as a novice rock climber, like rope-work, but staying safe on ice requires additional techniques.

As the name implies, mountaineering brings all these skills together on a mountain. But the difference is that while it's important to have the technical stuff nailed down, you also need a feel for mountain country, the kind of experience you can only get by spending time there. That was easy for me. I grew up in the mountains and spent my childhood roaming around them. Even as a child, working with the yaks, I knew what it was like to spend all day on my feet in rugged country with cloud swirling around the mountaintops, exposed to the cold. All of that is second nature to me. But mountain landscapes can be psychologically intimidating, even more so when they're at extreme altitude. What would be easy climbing at sea level in warm sunshine feels serious in the high mountains. That's why high-altitude mountaineering is the ultimate test of expertise and experience. It's also much more dangerous. Deaths do occur while rock climbing, but they are rare, certainly in comparison to Himalayan mountain climbing. For that reason, most rock climbers are happy to stay rock climbers and not bother with mountains, where life is tougher.

Sometimes it helps to think of mountains as weather factories, sticking up into the atmosphere and getting in the way of air streams. Understanding how weather impacts conditions on any mountain is a critical skill. They are often socked in with cloud, reducing visibility to zero. Strong winds can howl across summit ridges and blow you off balance – or leave you frozen and hypothermic. They can turn a leeward slope into an avalanche death trap. Some dangers are less obvious.

Ice can fracture unexpectedly as temperatures change. Rock on big mountains is often looser than on a cliff at sea level and needs care. Nobody wants a rock on the head. So technical skills, the ability to climb rock and ice, are only part of becoming a self-reliant, experienced mountaineer. Assessing risk is also part of the mix. Hopefully, you can now see why taking time to build up mountain experience is critical.

If all this sounds daunting then maybe that's no bad thing. Journalists in newspapers sometimes write that Everest is not so difficult. They should come and try. It's true, the first ascent was almost seventy years ago but the challenge is no less. It's the highest mountain on earth and the impact of such high altitude is always going to be extreme. And Everest is not a hike like Kilimanjaro: it's a serious mountaineering challenge. To climb it competently on your own without the support network that's put in place each spring would be an immense achievement. Very few of the very best high-altitude climbers have managed this. Reinhold Messner did it in 1980, without Sherpa support, fixed ropes or bottled oxygen. But then Reinhold Messner is one of the best high-altitude climbers of all time: ambitious, dedicated and very, very strong, both psychologically and physically.

So if you want to climb Everest, you have to be honest with yourself. Can I do it like Messner did? Do I have the time to become the kind of deeply experienced climber who can function with some margin of safety in such a hypoxic, or oxygen-deficient, environment? Very few people have the physiology and experience to climb Everest like that. So, in all likelihood, your answer to these questions is 'no'. Once you acknowledge you lack the experience to make decisions, manage supplies and equipment and keep yourself safe on your own, you're going to need a Sherpa guide, porters and fixed ropes to keep you safe. The companies that have the best success rates pay their high-altitude workers properly and have better logistics, all of which costs: this will be an expensive adventure. And don't think it won't still be incredibly tough. Don't think you won't curse yourself at times for taking on the challenge of Everest. But in bringing in some help, you've given yourself a much better chance.

CHAPTER TWO

The Challenge

When my father went to Everest in 1953, people still wondered if the mountain could be climbed. The first full attempt had been in 1922 from the Tibetan side along the north-east ridge from the North Col. Altogether there were seven expeditions from Tibet before the Second World War. After the war, on two expeditions in 1952, a team of very strong Swiss climbers got high on the mountain above the South Col, from the Nepali side, with Tenzing Norgay. When the British came the following year, they had the experience of the Swiss to draw on. They also brought Tenzing, who knew the route. They had done research into how the body works at high altitude and developed the best equipment available. What isn't mentioned so often is that the British were able to put more supplies of oxygen and equipment on the South Col than the Swiss. This was a big difference. And that was thanks to the Sherpa team who worked for them.

Since Tenzing and Sir Edmund Hillary reached the summit on 29 May 1953, up to the end of 2019, there have been over ten thousand ascents of Everest by almost six thousand people. Only 214 have done it without bottled oxygen: an exclusive club. Roughly half of the total ascents have been by foreign climbers, the rest by Sherpas and other hired workers. Almost a thousand Sherpas have climbed the mountain more than once. Thanks to decades of data collected by the American journalist Liz Hawley, we know that around two-thirds of ascents have been from the southern Nepal side of the mountain and a third from Tibet.

Over the years there have been many new and difficult routes climbed on Everest, but most climbers just want to get to the summit so they choose one of the two that are guided: the route the British tried from Tibet and the one Tenzing and Hillary climbed from

Nepal in 1953. Some guides will tell you they prefer the northern side, which doesn't have a dangerous icefall (I'll explain what that is later) to cross, but we're going to concentrate on the southern route, since that's most popular and has significant advantages.

Most likely, you'll be wondering how safe it is: what are my chances of not coming home? You're right to be worried. Climbing on Everest is almost a hundred years old and in that time 306 people have died on the mountain. Of those fatalities, 195 were on the Nepal side, roughly proportionate to the split in the number of climbers trying from the south and the north. Of the fourteen peaks over 8,000 metres, Everest certainly has the highest number of deaths, but that's because it's by far the most popular. It's better to look at the rate of fatalities. Statisticians have worked out two ways of illustrating this. One way is to correlate the number of people who climb above base camp to the number of deaths. It's currently around 1.17 deaths per hundred climbers on Everest. The worst rate is on Annapurna in central Nepal with a rate of 3.84 per hundred. You can also divide the number of total summits by the number of fatalities and express that as a percentage. On Everest that figure is 2.9 per cent. On Annapurna, it's nearer 25 per cent: for every four summits, one climber dies.

You must also remember that Everest has got *much* safer since guided climbing began in the 1990s. Before 1999, Everest was climbed 1,169 times and 170 people died, giving the much higher percentage of 14.9 per cent. The *current* rate is 1.5 per cent, although it must be said that figure is higher now than it was ten years ago, and for reasons I know only too well. In the early hours of 18 April 2014 I was dozing in my tent at base camp, at around 5,300 metres, half listening to the radio I keep near me when we have Sherpas from our team carrying loads up the mountain. Suddenly the radio burst into life. People were shouting with fear and horror. An ice cliff on the mountain's west shoulder had peeled off and thousands of tons of ice had fallen hundreds of feet on the Icefall, killing sixteen people, all of them high-altitude workers. Some of them were from my team, including my uncle Ang Tsering and his brother. That was a terrible day. My brother Lhakpa and I rushed up to the scene of the accident but there was nothing to be done. You can imagine what happens to a body that is hit with tons of ice. We found my uncle and his brother together, hand in hand, but we could only identify them from their boots. Three of the bodies were too deep to recover. Climbing on Everest was cancelled that season. Lhakpa said he wouldn't climb the mountain again, and he hasn't.

Despite my many years of climbing Everest, that was the first time someone so close to me was killed. That it happened in the Icefall was no surprise, especially to us Sherpas. It is the first leg on the route to the summit and for us the most dangerous. It's also our workplace. Now, because I'm a guide, I don't carry loads through the Icefall but lots of young Sherpas do. To understand why it's so dangerous, you have to understand what the Icefall is: a glacier flowing from the basin below the mountain, which tumbles over a steep slope in the rock beneath. As it goes over the lip, like water in rapids, it fractures and splits, forming crevasses and unstable ice blocks. It's the job of a team of Sherpas called the Icefall Doctors to find a route through this maze each spring and fix it with rope and ladders for the clients that follow. Each season it has changed as ice has shifted and fallen. When you're in it, you can hear creaks and cracks as the ice moves. When I was a young Sherpa, going through it for the first time, I can admit I was a little bit frightened.

This stretch of the climb takes you from base camp on the Khumbu glacier to camp one on the lip of the Western Cwm, above the Icefall. That's a height gain of around 600 metres in little more than a mile and a half. Depending on how fit and acclimatised you are it will take three to six hours. The Icefall is safer at night, before the sun gets to work raising the temperature, so we get up at around 3 a.m. and start climbing as soon as we can. Camp one is only there for part of the season, to help clients acclimatise and as a staging post to camp two, which is another two hours and another mile and a half deeper into the Western Cwm. This section is heavily crevassed but less chaotic than the Icefall. The problem here can be heat: it gets surprisingly hot with the sun reflecting off the snow. Camp two is under the mountain's south-west face at an altitude of 6,400 metres and is much more comfortable, with a cook to make dinner, everything from our local *dal bhat*, lentils and rice, to spaghetti carbonara, and plenty of room to rest.

Above camp two, the angle steepens sharply under the summit of Lhotse, Everest's near neighbour. This slope is called the Lhotse face and there's a third camp in the middle of it, just above an area of crevasses at around 7,200 metres. That's a height gain of 800 metres in a mile and a half. The route will be well prepared, with a fixed rope to follow and steps in the snow already kicked, but it's steep ground and people can and do die in falls from here. It's important to stay clipped to the ropes. The altitude also begins to bite hard on this section. I promise you by the time you get there you'll be feeling it. The fourth camp is another 600 metres above you, on the South Col itself, exposed to savage winds, the launching pad for the climb to the South Summit and the spectacular ridge beyond that to the summit itself: this is the most exposed part of the climb. Just below the top is the feature known as the Hillary Step, although the earthquake that struck the region in 2015 has altered its shape, making it easier to climb.

Just as there is on the rest of the route, there is fixed rope here to keep you secure, something Tenzing and Hillary didn't have in 1953.

Everest has not only got safer, but the proportion of climbers reaching the summit has also gone up. Twenty years ago there were expeditions that didn't get anyone to the top. Now, if you're aged between thirty-five and fifty, the likelihood of you succeeding is more than eighty per cent. Even if you are older than that, it's still better than fifty-fifty. Why am I giving you those ages? That's because the most common demographic on Everest is middle-aged men who have had time to build sufficient personal wealth to spend $50,000 and upwards on a climbing holiday. A far greater proportion of these men now come from Asian countries, particularly China and India. There are also more women these days; there have been 702 summits by women.

Why are so many more people succeeding on Everest? Has it got easier? No. It's still the huge challenge it always was. What has changed is how we climb it. In the quarter century that it has been offered as a commercial peak, guides on Everest have learned a lot.

Those lessons can be distilled into two words: 'more' and 'better'. Equipment, everything from the quality of boots to oxygen regulators, is better. Weather forecasts are much better. And there's more support: more fixed rope and above all more Sherpas and other high-altitude workers. The numbers of Sherpas supporting clients has gone up markedly over the last twenty years, carrying more oxygen bottles up the mountain which in turn means clients can breathe oxygen at a faster rate.

I can tell you that if you set your sights on Everest, you prepare well and you commit, you've got a good chance of reaching the top. Are you ready to start?

CHAPTER THREE

Preparing for Everest

When people ask me how to prepare for Everest, they are usually thinking about their physical condition and ways to improve it. They'll say: do you train? And the honest answer is no. I'm usually active and usually in the mountains, if not climbing then trekking. So my body is in good shape, even as I turn fifty. That doesn't mean I don't suffer. People think, because of our genetic adaptations, that Sherpas find Everest easy, but we don't. We might find it easier, but that's a different thing. We still suffer. Even for Sherpas it's difficult. If I was going to recommend a path to readying yourself for such a big climb, then I think it comes down to two phrases: 'mental toughness' and 'humility to learn'. Let's start with the humility bit.

When I started climbing Everest in my early twenties, there was no instruction course for me to learn basic techniques such as using an ice axe and crampons, rope-work, or keeping myself safe using the 'jumar' clamps[3] on a fixed rope. I simply asked the older Sherpas around me and learned fast because my life depended on it. Much later, more than a decade after my first summit in 1994, the American climber Conrad Anker and some of his friends opened a climbing school for Sherpas in the off-season. By then I'd been working for the American guiding outfit AAI for several years. You might say I was at the top of my game. But I was so eager to take the course; in fact, I went three years running. By then I knew the techniques I needed very well but I wanted to learn how to teach them to others. How could I train beginners without those skills? I also wanted to learn first aid, and to gain a better understanding of the physiological pitfalls of high altitude. I didn't know everything. I wanted to learn and get better. And I still do.

It's easy when you know nothing to have that attitude. You're a beginner: you're not supposed to know anything. As your experience and ability grows, it gets harder. The years pass and you have some success. When less experienced climbers start talking about what they can do, it's tempting to smile and think you have nothing to learn. But it's not true. Just because we see ourselves as experts in something doesn't mean we've earned the right to be close-minded. Because the mountain doesn't know you're an expert. So before you start, prepare yourself to maintain your humility. It may just save your life.

If you've got the ambition to climb Everest, chances are you already have a passion for mountains. You ski, or hike, or run in them. You're also probably quite fit. Keep doing your regular workout, but remember that even if you're being guided and supported, Everest requires a particular skill set and type of fitness and you'll have to acquire both.

We can break preparation down into three areas: technique, fitness and psychology. If you're already rock climbing then you're ahead of the game. Although, as we've seen in my overview of the route, there isn't much rock climbing to be done, taking a course in easy rock climbing or scrambling attunes your body and mind to the process of moving up steep ground using arms as well as legs. It makes you more balanced for climbing. Wherever you are in the world, there will be someone competent and safe to offer you instruction in this. Most countries have climbing organisations that can offer advice on where to go. Learn how to rock climb somewhere warm and sunny, so it's a pleasure. You'll be plenty cold enough later on.

Once you're comfortable climbing high above the ground on rock, you can move on to climbing snow and ice. If you ski, then snow will feel very familiar. But there's a great deal to learn about climbing in crampons and glacier travel that is hugely relevant to climbing Everest. There are stories about climbers arriving at base camp needing to be taught how to put their crampons on. Don't be one of them. Camping in sub-zero temperatures is also something you shouldn't experience for the first time just before you start your ascent. You'll be at base camp for months and learning how to be comfortable beforehand takes the pressure off psychologically.

As well as learning the ropes, you'll need to work

on your stamina. Start with a visit to your doctor for a health check, with particular attention on how your lungs and heart perform. There's only a third of the oxygen we're used to high on Everest, so your lungs and heart are sorely tested. If there's a problem you need to know now, not after you reach the mountain. You'll read that most people lose weight on a long expedition. That's true, but don't be tempted to put on lots of weight before the climb to compensate: rather, try to eat well at base camp. There are useful training programmes now available to help you but it's good to spend whole days in the mountains. This need only be hiking, or with scrambling thrown in, but build up so you're spending longer and longer periods on your feet, climbing and descending. The summit day on Everest can last twelve to fifteen hours, starting at 11 p.m. at night, after three days or more of climbing, and in a hypoxic, freezing environment. Get used to being exhausted and cold. Very few of us reach the limits of our physical capability; our minds stop us long before that. Keep pushing back that envelope of tolerance until a fifteen-hour day after no sleep is something you can manage.

Climbing some big mountains away from Everest will help this process. Aconcagua, for example, is a great objective: not technically demanding, but at almost 7,000 metres high it's a good intermediary altitude on the road to Everest. You won't be climbing higher than this on Everest without oxygen, so it gives you the opportunity to test how you react to altitude and how you acclimatise. Above all, I recommend climbing mountains in Nepal. There are trekking peaks in the Everest region of Khumbu, where I did my first guiding, like Mera and Island Peak that are over 6,000 metres. These are a great start. But I'd also recommend climbing something more substantial in Nepal before going to Everest; something over 7,000 metres will give you more confidence. The better Everest guiding companies offer a pathway for those whose ultimate dream is to climb Everest and many of these options will be part of their programme.

What I stress above all is psychological resilience: grit. Getting in physical shape for Everest is tough. Being mentally strong enough is even tougher. Growing up in the mountains and fighting to make something of myself was good preparation. When I'm on Everest I'm totally focused. I tell clients they have to commit to what they're doing. Many climbers suffer ill health: bad stomachs or a persistent cough, known as the 'Khumbu cough'. That can chip away at their confidence. There's a lot of downtime in an Everest expedition: lots of time alone in your tent to think. You get anxious. It's natural to miss your family when you're at base camp for so long. But if you get homesick, then you won't want to climb. If you want to climb Everest then it's essential to put all that to one side and make the mountain your home instead.

Now buckle up, because it's time to climb.

CHAPTER FOUR

The Climb

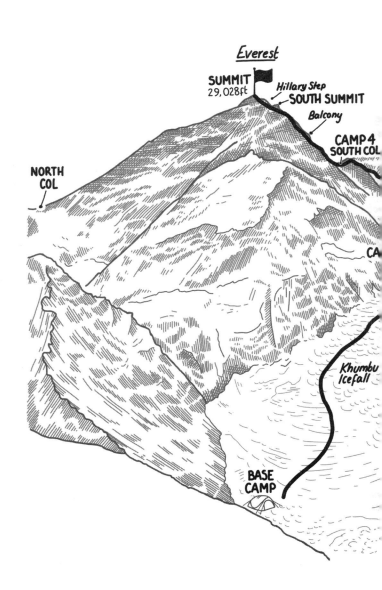

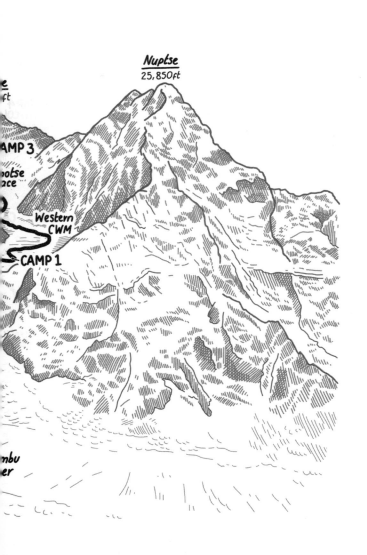

Nuptse
25,850ft

CAMP 3

otse
ce

Western
CWM

CAMP 1

mbu
er

My expedition starts in March a few weeks before yours: setting up base camp and starting work on the route through the Icefall all happen before you arrive in Nepal. The main thing you have to focus on is reaching Kathmandu in great shape and staying that way. It's a bit crazy as we're surrounded by the purest air in the mountains, but the city's air quality is not the best. We like to joke we're used to it, but it's really no laughing matter. You don't want to arrive at base camp with a lung or gastrointestinal infection that you can't shake off. Take care of yourself, relax and try not to think too far ahead. You're still at least six weeks from the summit.

The flight into Lukla, where you start trekking to base camp, is one of the most exciting in the world. You think you're flying into a mountain before you spot the short runway, like the deck of an aircraft carrier and at quite an angle. If you love flying, enjoy; if you don't, remember the pilots are hugely experienced on this sector: up to fifty flights a day land here in season. Once on the ground take a deep breath of air. At 2,800 metres, it's the lowest you're going to be for the next two months. Base camp is still two and a half kilometres higher and a lot colder: there's no rush to get there, so take your time. Your guiding company will have figured out the best schedule based on their experience of how clients react to altitude, but if you need more time, then take it.

Acclimatisation is a mysterious business and the physiology of it is still being studied. We don't have all the answers. I'm lucky: I have the very specific adaptations that give Tibetans their edge at altitude. Our metabolism uses oxygen more efficiently than the rest of humanity. But we are adapted to altitudes of 4,000 metres, not 8,000, so above base camp we suffer too. In someone without that advantage, lower oxygen prompts your body to breathe harder and your heart to beat faster. During the few weeks of acclimatisation, your bone marrow starts to produce more red blood cells, making your blood 'stickier', meaning it can clot more easily. Staying hydrated is critically important. Your body's cells also become more efficient, something they achieve by focusing less on repair and more on energy output. That's why injuries at altitude can take much longer to heal. What's certain is that everybody is different in how they acclimatise, but you've done some big mountains now and you will know what your body needs.

The trek takes around ten days, sometimes less, and you'll be at base camp by mid-April. I urge you to enjoy the mountains as you walk in. Enjoy the life around you. Base camp is a tough place to live and you can feel the pressure building as weeks pass and you get close to the summit climb. The first thing we do, after settling everyone in, is to hold the expedition *puja*, or prayer ceremony. Many Sherpas were novice monks as boys, so we know the ritual off by heart, but we often get an ordained lama from the monastery at Tengboche or elsewhere to come and give his blessing to the climbers and their gear. Incense is burned and offerings made, and colourful prayer flags strung across base camp. People often wonder what the ceremony means and ask whether we really believe it brings us good luck. I say that no *puja* ceremony is going to stop an avalanche.

But the prayers put us in the right psychological space: focused and ready, and humble too. After all, this is the abode of the gods.

For the next month, you will be adjusting to the altitude and making sure you're comfortable with the techniques you'll be using on the mountain: crossing ladders, using fixed ropes, rappelling, or using a brake to slide down the rope, and walking in crampons. This includes travelling a short way into the Icefall so you'll be used to its strangeness, all the creaks and crashes of the lower glacier, before going any further. Crossing a crevasse on a ladder takes practice; you've got a fixed rope to keep you safe, but balancing in big heavy boots with crampons can feel precarious. Take time to build your confidence so you can move through this dangerous area efficiently.

After that we begin a sequence of excursions up the mountain, sleeping progressively higher and spending more time up there. We call these rotations. There's no hard and fast rule about the sequence of these, but one common pattern is to climb to camp one at 5,900 metres and descend, then climb to camp one and sleep. Next day you might climb up to camp two at 6,400 metres and then return to camp one for a second night. If you're going well, you might then move up to camp two and spend a couple of nights there before descending for a rest at base camp. Then you take a long rest, four days or more, eating and sleeping, before going up for your second rotation: up to camp one, then camp two and then, if all's well, up to camp three at 7,200 metres. Your guides will make a decision about whether or not to spend the night here depending on conditions. After that, it's back down to base camp for more rest. Many climbers choose to drop down below base camp to a lower altitude to rest and eat, ready for the summit climbing.

By the middle of May, your summit attempt is getting close. Thanks to the excellent forecasts we now have, your guide will have a clear idea of when the summit windows will be, as winds moderate ahead of the monsoon. Sometimes there might only be a day or two, which is when you'll see pictures of queues of climbers close to the summit. That's because everyone is funnelled into those dates. But while the newspapers get excited, it's worth saying that Everest is a lot less busy than many peaks in the Alps, like Mont Blanc or the Matterhorn. Normally, the weather gods are kinder and more summit days are available, spreading numbers out.

With a good weather report, you'll start your journey to the summit, climbing through the Icefall for the last time straight to camp two and take a rest day before continuing to camp three. Assuming the weather remains stable, we'll now put on the oxygen gear. (Some climbers start using it earlier.) Climbing with a mask on your face can take some adjustment, but don't worry: you'll have experienced this already during the period of acclimatisation.

Above camp three, the route is unfamiliar and pretty steep. Many climbers will already be thinking about the long summit day coming up, but it's important to focus on the challenges immediately in front of you. This isn't such a long day and to take the edge off the low temperature we leave the tent just after sunrise. After an hour or so of steep snow slopes you reach what's called the Yellow Band, a section of marble between the upper slopes of limestone and the granite core of the mountain. This isn't so steep but you'll feel the benefit of fixed ropes here, climbing rock in crampons. Not far from the South Col itself is another, steeper section of rock which requires focus. This section of the route will only get rockier as climate change strips ice and snow off the face. And once the sun gets up you won't believe you were ever cold.

You can expect to be in camp four at around 8 a.m. or 9 a.m. and you have the rest of the day to relax and rest, take in the stupendous position you find yourself in, drink as much as you can and prepare yourself for the night ahead. It's windy here, but if you're managing to sleep, your Sherpa guide will wake you around 9 p.m. with some fluids and you'll get ready to leave, zipping up your down suit, putting your boots and crampons back on, then your harness, and making sure your oxygen is working. Assuming you're climbing with the best guiding outfits, you'll be using four litres per minute. Your Sherpa guide will be carrying spare bottles of gas for you, as well as their own. They'll be using something like one and half litres per minute.

The slopes above the South Col are some of the steepest on the mountain and you're isolated by the darkness, climbing in the pool of your headlamp. Adrenaline will be flooding your system, but it's important to get a rhythm going as best as you are able. It's a long time until dawn and you've got a lot of ground to cover: it's something like a mile from the South Col to the summit and around 850 metres of height gain. After the initial steep slopes you reach a feature known as the Balcony, a flatter area where you can rest and change oxygen bottles. In terms of height gain, you're about halfway to the summit, at around 8,400 metres.

Above the Balcony, your world begins to open out. Day is breaking; the mountains glow pink with that haunting light that transforms the mountains just before the sun appears. Behind you is the summit of Lhotse, and behind that is the stunning peak of Makalu. Both are now beneath you. The slopes here are easy enough but then they steepen and become rocky, especially the last hundred feet or so to the South Summit, where you get your first sight of the final summit ridge. This isn't so difficult but is what climbers call exposed, meaning there are big drops at your feet. Focus hard on what you're doing and each step you take. This ridge brings you to the famous Hillary Step, the last difficult obstacle between you and the summit. You have the rope to keep you safe, pushing the clamp ahead of you and stepping up, keeping your feet apart for stability, and it's soon past. The situation though is incredible. Above this, the ridge continues in a series of bumps to the summit itself after around half an hour of effort. You'll recognise the top by the prayer flags and the throng of very happy climbers standing on it. Don't worry: it's big enough for you too.

We started with me on the summit of Everest. We finish with you there. How does it feel? People often ask me whether I enjoy my job and I tell them I do, but not for the climbing. I've done Everest before and I don't need to do it again. I enjoy my job because of what I see in the faces of the people I guide right at this moment, when they reach the top. I do it because

I get to meet amazing people from all over the world and watch them realise their dream. You could be one of them. But even if you never get near the real Everest, there's still the opportunity to climb your own Everest. Don't let it go.

Notes

1   A col is a saddle or lowest point on a ridge between two peaks. Everest has two famous ones, on the north side and the south.
2   Tenzing Norgay was one of the first two people to reach the summit of Mount Everest. He accomplished this with Edmund Hillary on 29 May 1953.
3   A jumar or ascender is a device that can slide up a rope but won't slide down. On Everest, it's a way of protecting a climber and helping them climb as well.